ROCK & POP

Grade 8
GUITAR

TRINITY
COLLEGE LONDON

THE EXAM AT A GLANCE

For your Rock & Pop exam you will need to perform a set of **three songs** and one of the **Session skills** assessments, either **Playback** or **Improvising**. You can choose the order in which you play your set-list.

Song 1

Choose a song from this book

OR from www.trinityrock.com

Song 2

Choose a different song from this book

OR from www.trinityrock.com

OR perform a song you have chosen yourself: this could be your own cover version or a song you have written. It should be at the same level as the songs in this book. See the website for detailed requirements.

Song 3: Technical focus

Choose one of the Technical focus songs from this book, which cover three specific technical elements.

Session skills

Choose either **Playback** or **Improvising**.

When you are preparing for your exam please check on **www.trinityrock.com** for the most up-to-date information and requirements as these can change from time to time.

CONTENTS

Tuning track 1: E, A, D, G, B, E with a pause between each note.

Tuning track 2: D, A, D, G, B, E (for song requiring detuned D).

Trinity College London's Rock & Pop syllabus and supporting publications have been devised and produced in association with Faber Music and Peters Edition London.

Trinity College London
Registered office:
89 Albert Embankment
London SE1 7TP UK
T + 44 (0)20 7820 6100
F + 44 (0)20 7820 6161
E music@trinitycollege.co.uk
www.trinitycollege.co.uk

Registered in the UK. Company no. 02683033
Charity no. 1014792
Patron HRH The Duke of Kent KG

Copyright © 2012 Trinity College London
3rd impression, March 2013

Cover and book design by Chloë Alexander
Brand development by Andy Ashburner @ Caffeinehit (www.caffeinehit.com)
Photographs courtesy of Rex Features Ltd
Photograph of Eddie Hazel by Gilles Petard/Redferns
Printed in England by Caligraving Ltd
Audio produced, mixed and mastered by Tom Fleming
Guitar arranged by Tom Fleming
Backing tracks arranged by Tom Fleming
Musicians
Vocals: Bo Walton
Keyboards: Dave Maric
Guitar: Tom Fleming & Steve Pigott
Bass: Ben Hillyard & Tom Fleming
Drums: George Double
Studio Engineer: Joel Davies www.thelimehouse.com

ISBN: 978-0-85736-226-1

SONGS FREEWILL

Rush
Words and Music by Geddy Lee, Neil Peart and Alex Lifeson

Lyrics under staff:

You can choose from phan-tom fears and kind-ness that can kill.

I will choose a path that's clear, I will choose free will.

Link

Guitar solo

Dm

f with distortion boost
1° play as written, 2° improvise (build)

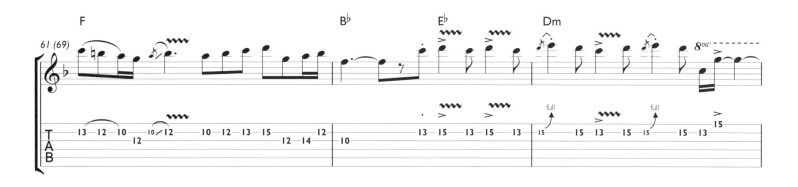

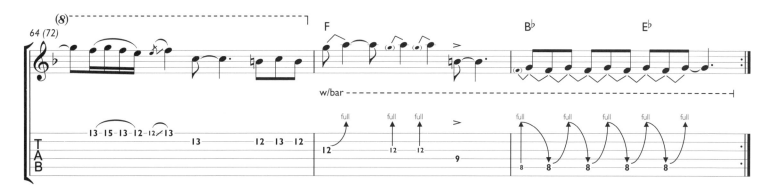

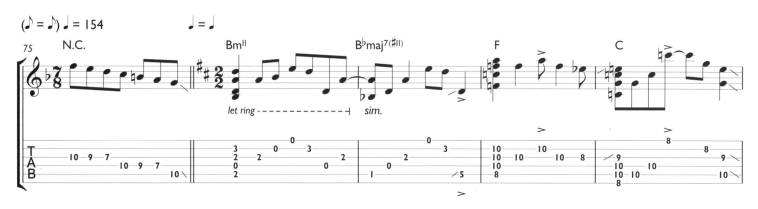

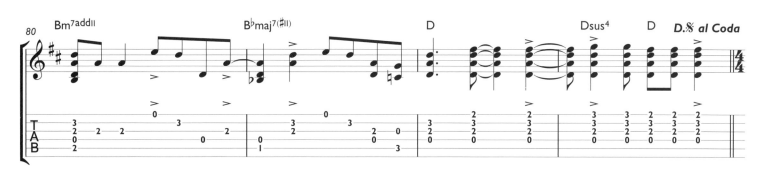

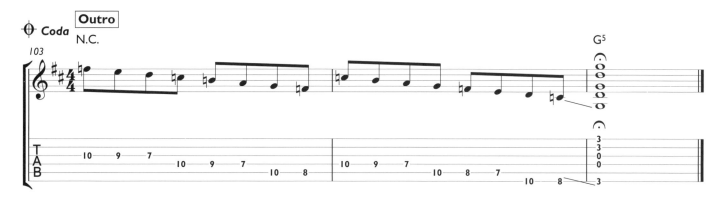

SONGS RUN TO THE HILLS

Iron Maiden
Words and Music by Stephen Harris

♩ = 120 **Classic Rock** *2 bars count-in*

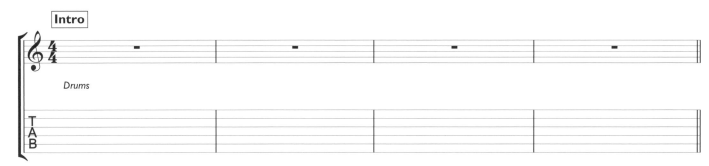

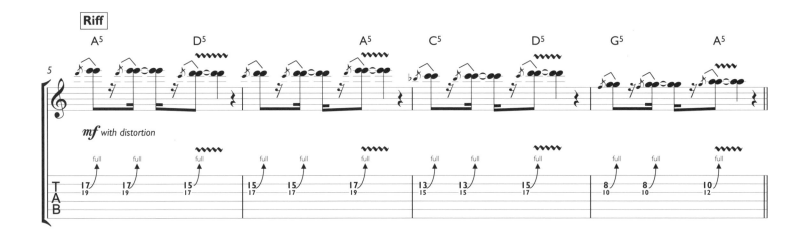

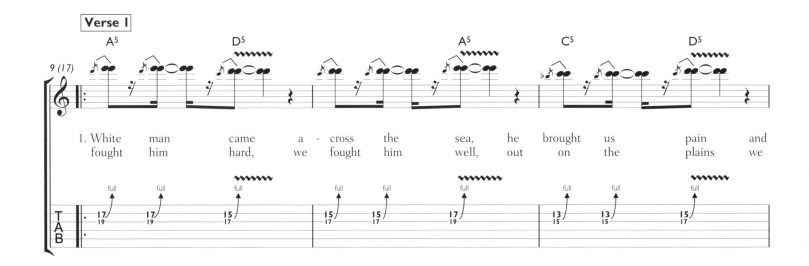

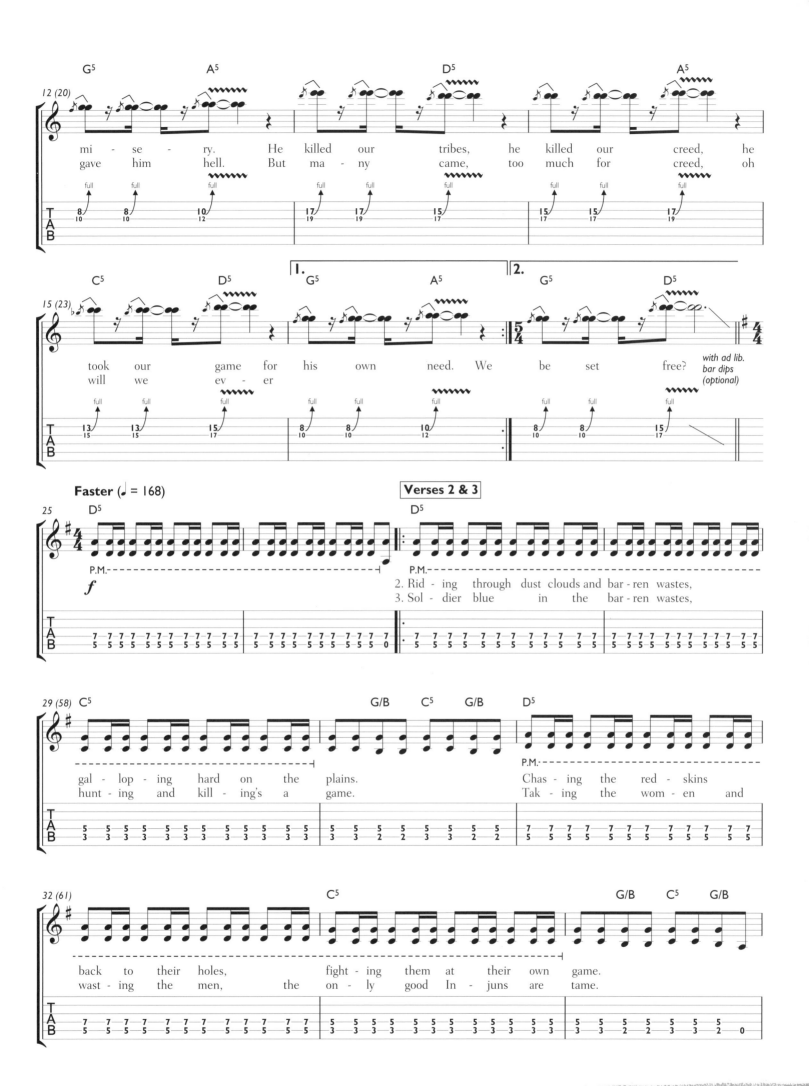

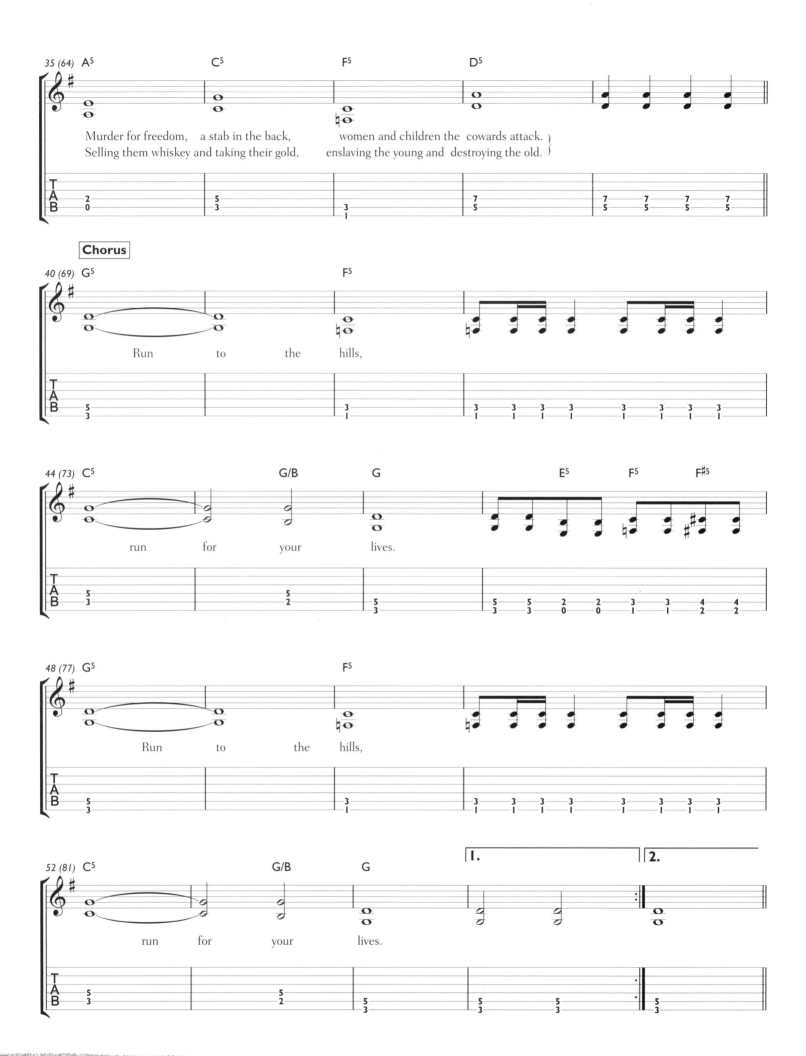

Murder for freedom, a stab in the back,   women and children the cowards attack.
Selling them whiskey and taking their gold, enslaving the young and destroying the old.

Chorus

Run   to   the   hills,

run   for   your   lives.

Run   to   the   hills,

run   for   your   lives.

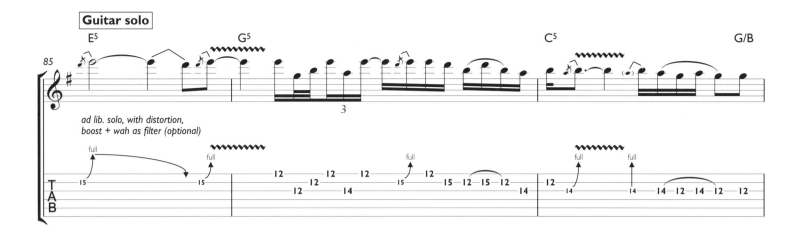

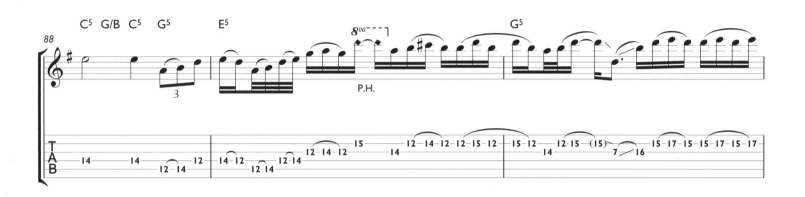

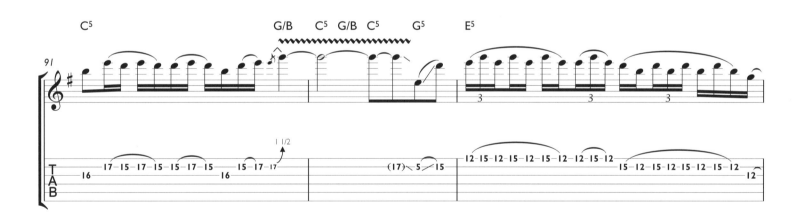

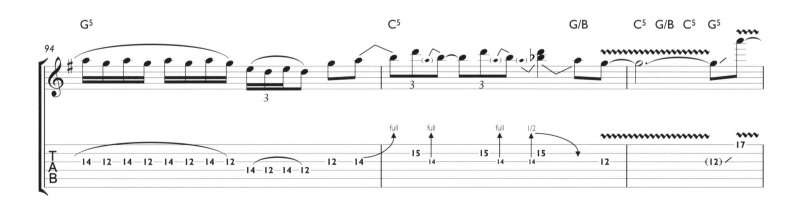

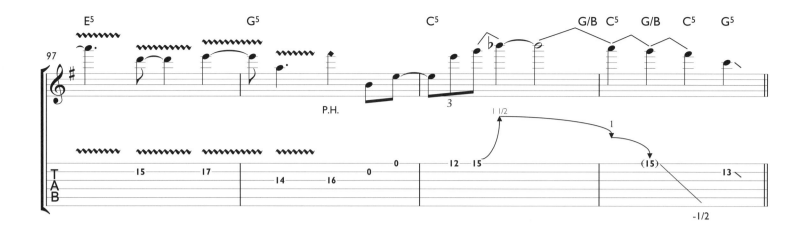

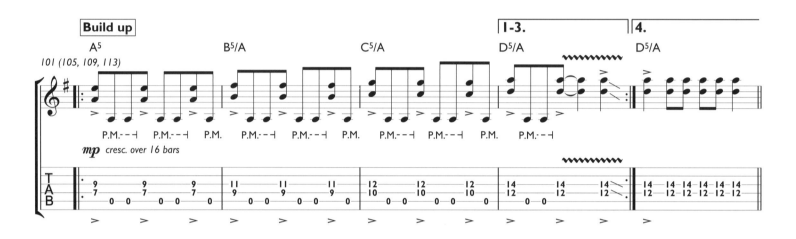

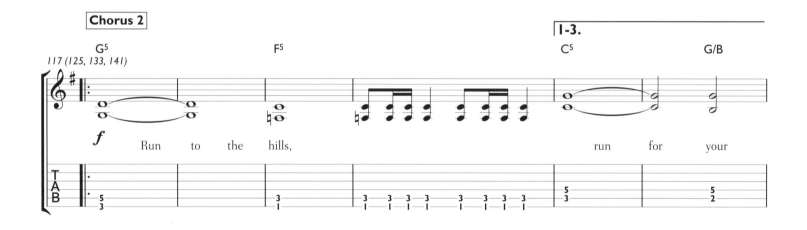

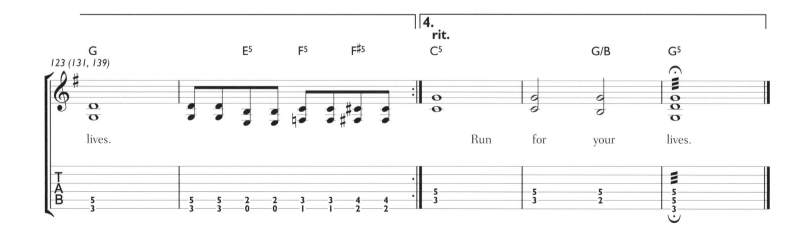

SONGS MAGGOT BRAIN

Funkadelic
Words and Music by George Clinton Jr and Eddie Hazel

♩. = 48 **Psychedelic Rock**   *2 bars count-in*

Intro

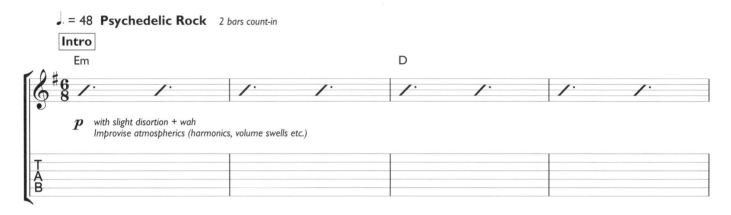

p with slight disortion + wah
Improvise atmospherics (harmonics, volume swells etc.)

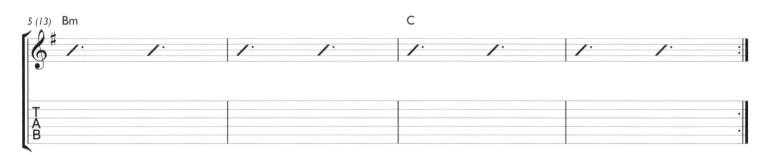

Theme

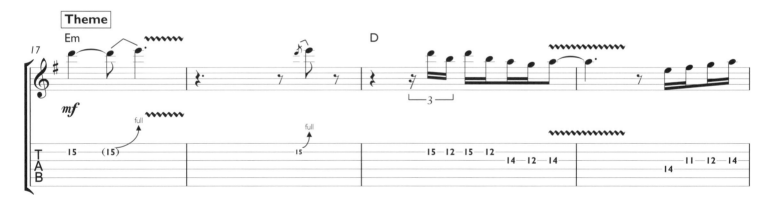

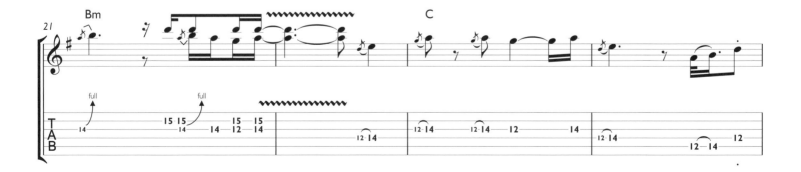

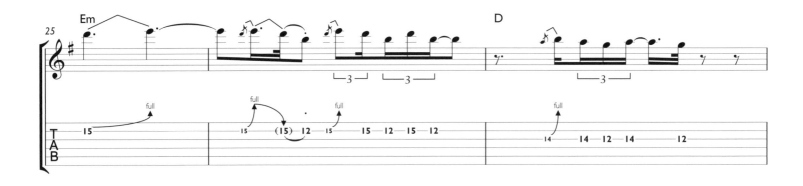

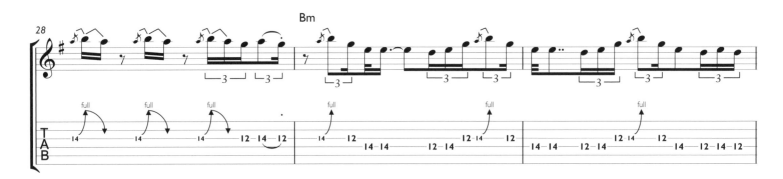

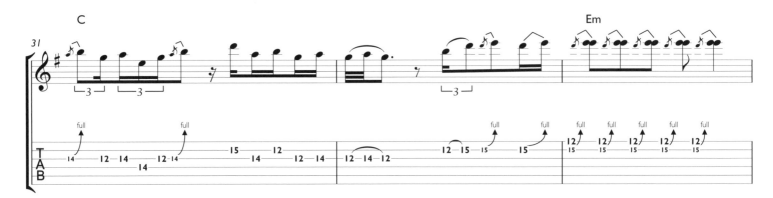

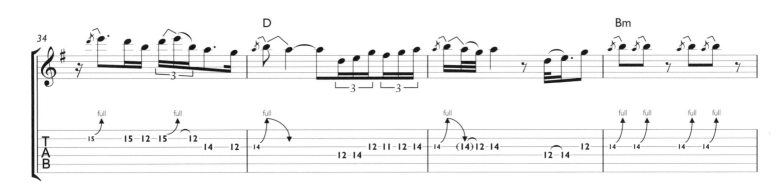

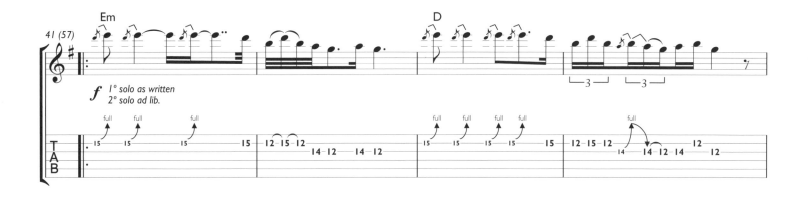

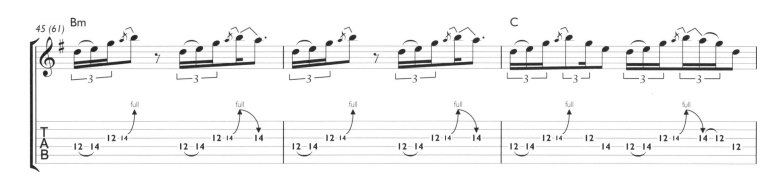

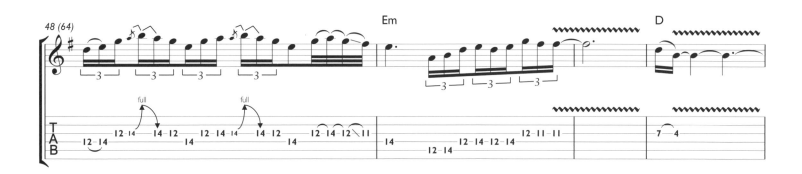

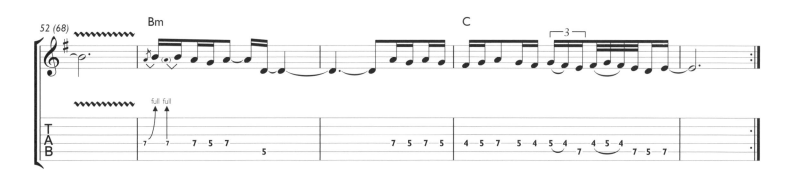

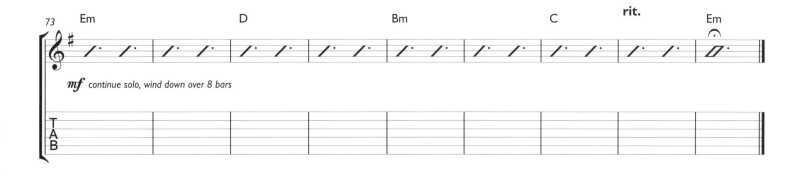

SONGS 6:00

Dream Theater
Words and Music by John Petrucci, Kevin Moore, Michael Portnoy,
John Myung and Kevin James LaBrie

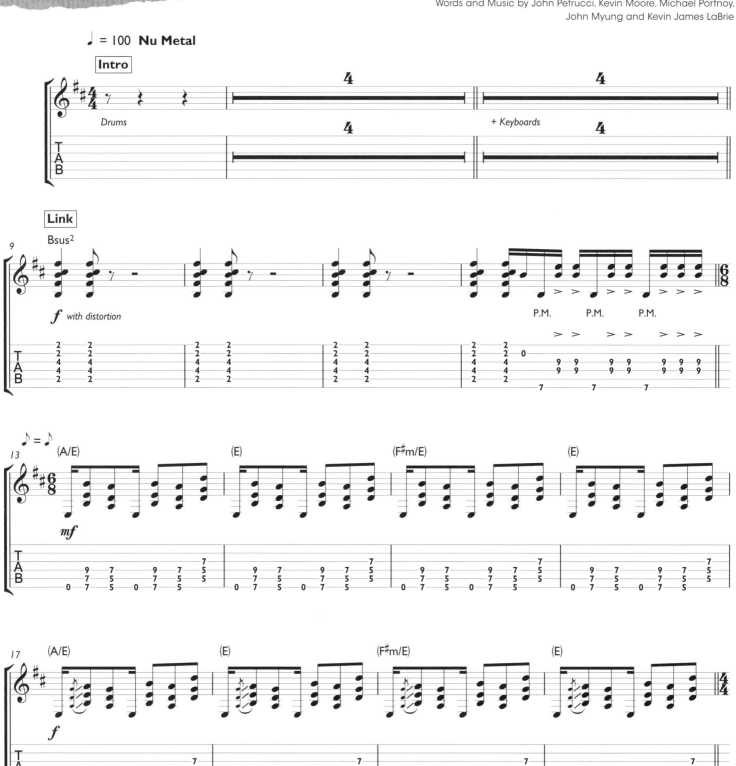

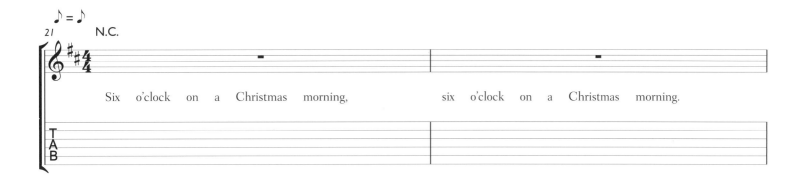

Six o'clock on a Christmas morning, six o'clock on a Christmas morning.

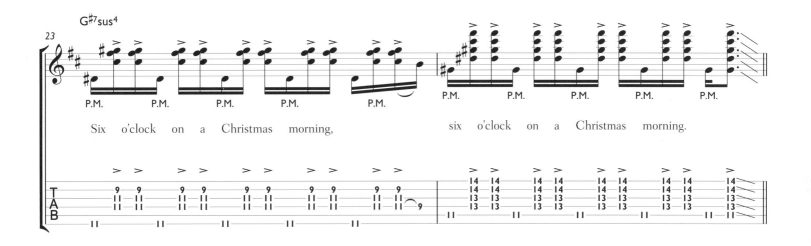

Six o'clock on a Christmas morning, six o'clock on a Christmas morning.

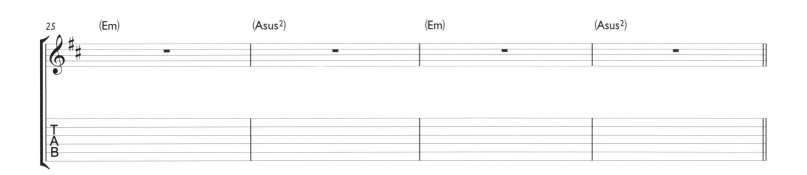

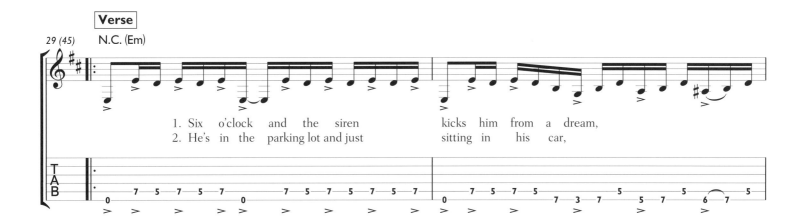

Verse

1. Six o'clock and the siren kicks him from a dream,
2. He's in the parking lot and just sitting in his car,

he tries to shake it off but it just won't stop
it's nine o'clock but he can't get out.

can't find the strength but he's got promises to keep,
He lights a cigarette and turns the music down,

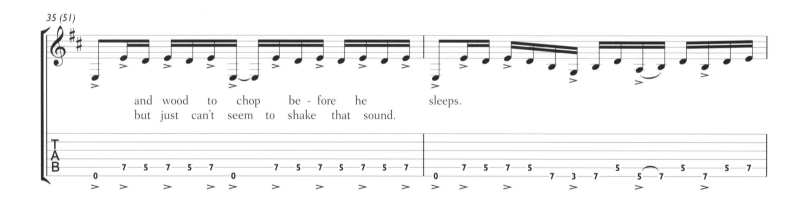

and wood to chop be-fore he sleeps.
but just can't seem to shake that sound.

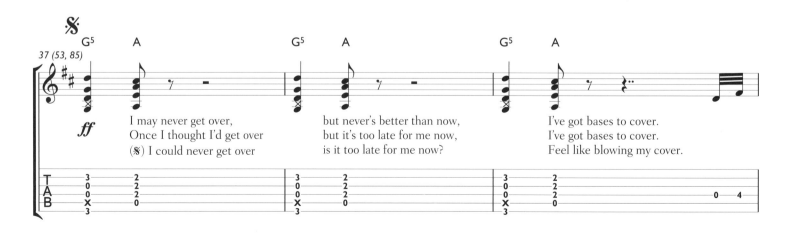

| G5 | A | G5 | A | G5 | A |

I may never get over,
Once I thought I'd get over
(%) I could never get over

but never's better than now,
but it's too late for me now,
is it too late for me now?

I've got bases to cover.
I've got bases to cover.
Feel like blowing my cover.

1.

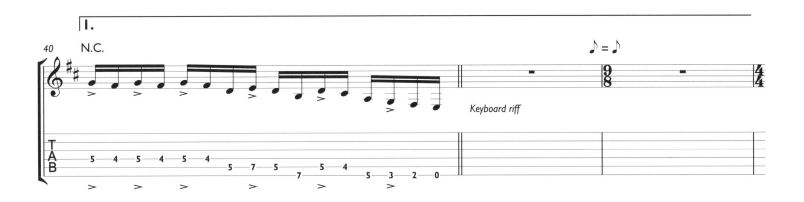

Keyboard riff

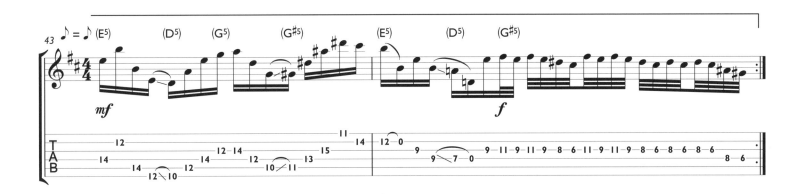

2, 3. **Chorus**

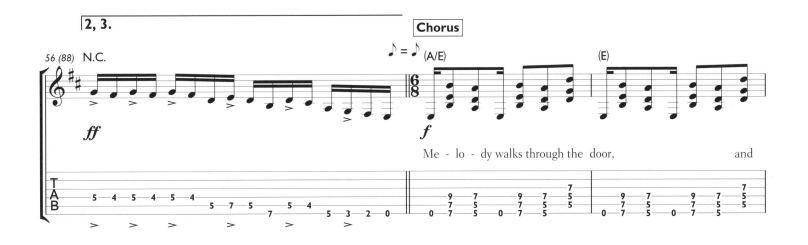

Me - lo - dy walks through the door, and

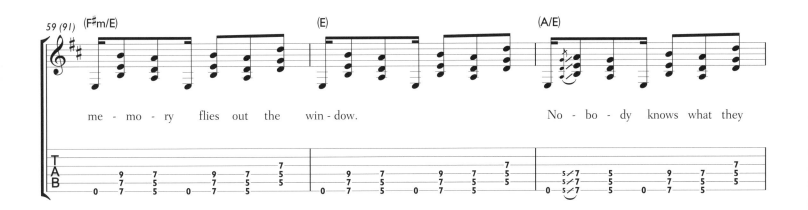

me - mo - ry flies out the win - dow. No - bo - dy knows what they

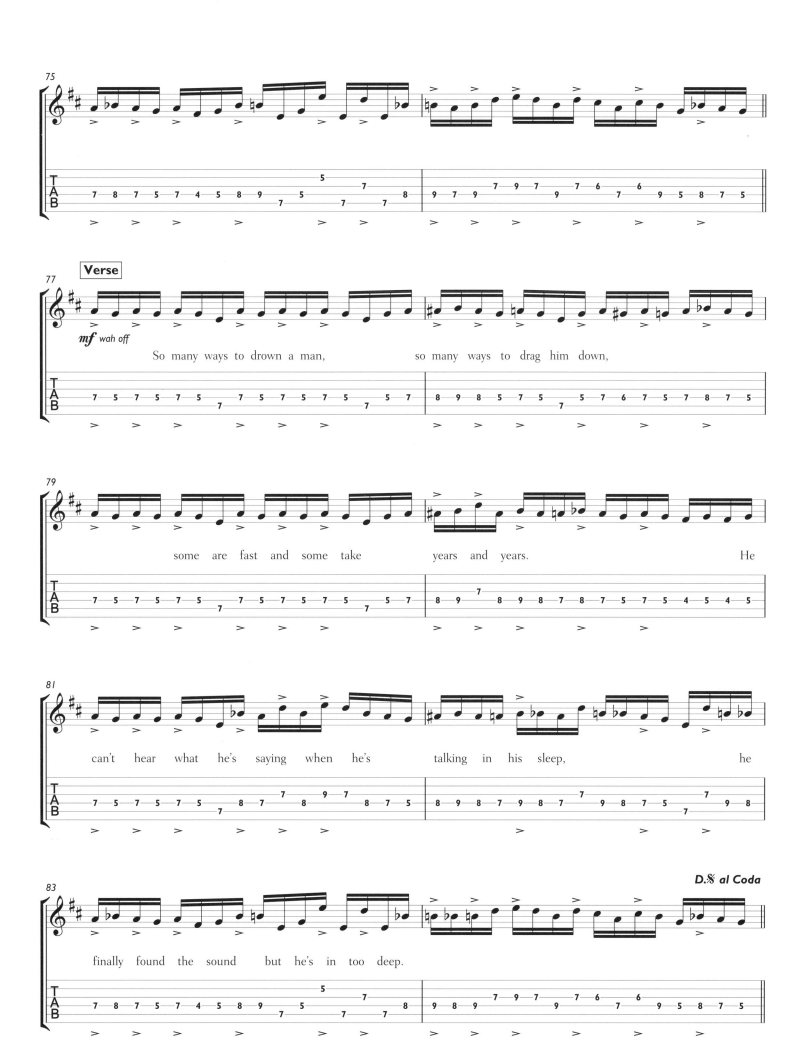

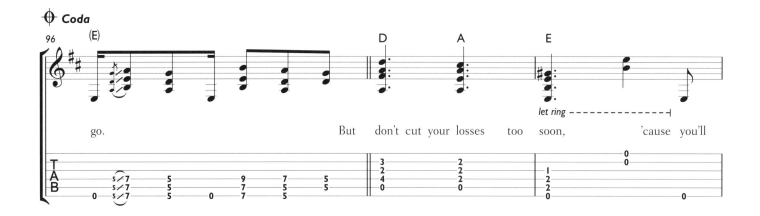

go. But don't cut your losses too soon, 'cause you'll

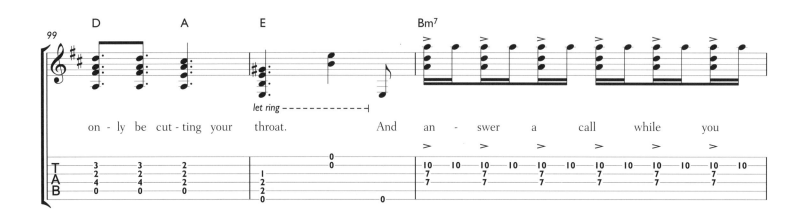

on - ly be cut - ting your throat. And an - swer a call while you

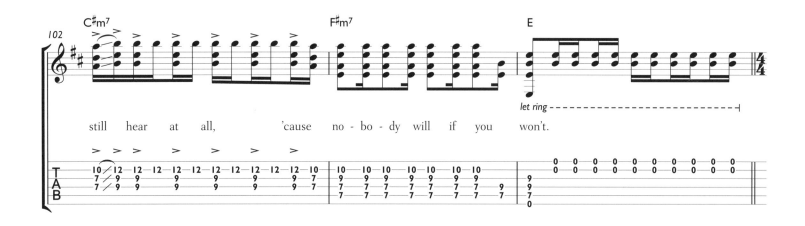

still hear at all, 'cause no - bo - dy will if you won't.

Outro

Six o'clock on a Christmas morning, six o'clock on a Christmas morning.

Big Drum fill

THE CRYING MACHINE

In your exam, you will be assessed on the following technical elements:

1 Bends (including unison bends)

'The Crying Machine' incorporates several different types of string bend. It is important that all notes are played in tune and reach their target pitch. As well as standard tone (in bar 1, for example) and semitone bends (in bar 8, for example), there are unison bends in bar 44. To play these, the two notes should be struck simultaneously, bending the lower notes up to the pitch of the higher notes. Be sure to reach a true unison – otherwise they will sound dissonant.

2 Improvising a solo

In bars 46–61 there is an opportunity to improvise a guitar solo. Make sure that you stay within the given style using, for example, unison bends, trills, pinch harmonics, bar vibrato, dips and dive bombs. You can write and memorise your solo, or improvise it in the exam. Aim to make your improvisation develop in a logical and interesting way, as well as following the chord symbols.

3 *Legato* technique

Legato technique is important in section 3 of the written solo. In each of the slurred phrases, only the first note should be struck. The notes are connected by hammer-ons, pull-offs and *legato* slides. Aim for a smooth and fluid sound.

THE CRYING MACHINE

Steve Vai
Words and Music by Steve Vai

TRACK 11 demo   TRACK 12 backing

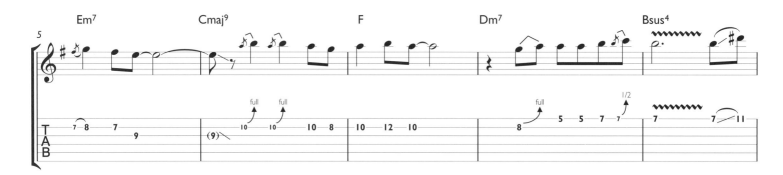

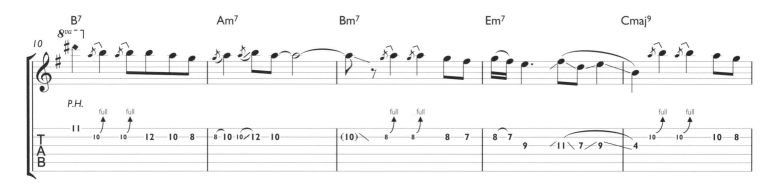

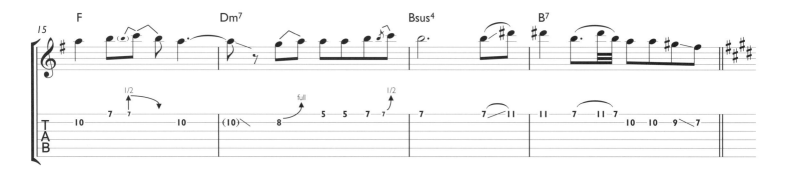

H *All slurred groups indicate continuous LH legato using HO/PO technique and slides if indicated – RH strikes first note only*

YOUR PAGE

NOTES

5150

In your exam, you will be assessed on the following technical elements:

1 Pinch harmonics

Pinch harmonics are used in bars 77 and 85. They are marked in the score by diamond noteheads and the letters P.H. Pick the string, then lightly bring the side of your thumb (or index finger) down onto the string, taking care not to mute it. Aim for a strong, high-pitched sound.

2 Improvising a solo

You are given the opportunity to improvise the second part of the solo, starting at bar 101. Make sure that you stay within the given style using, for example, right-hand tapping, pinch harmonics, bar vibrato, dips and dive bombs. You can write and memorise your solo, or improvise it in the exam. Aim to make your solo develop in a logical and interesting way, as well as following the chord symbols.

3 Whammy bar techniques

'5150' incorporates several whammy bar techniques such as bar vibrato, dips (bars 47–48, for example) and dive bombs (bar 25, for example). Take care with the intonation and make sure that you reach the target notes as indicated.

5150

Van Halen
Words and Music by Alex Van Halen, Edward Van Halen,
Michael Anthony and Sammy Hagar

Guitar in drop D tuning
(tune lowest string down to D)

♩ = 156 **Classic Rock** *2 bars count-in*

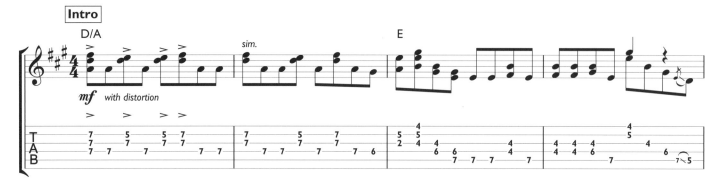

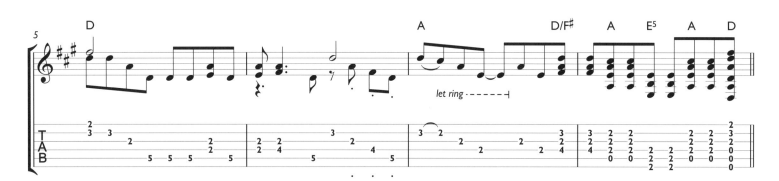

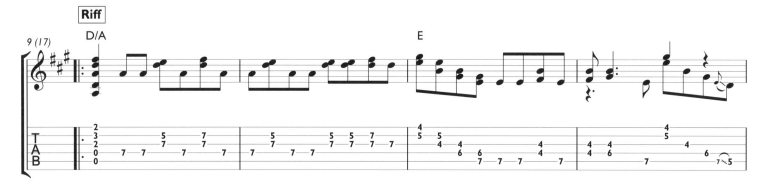

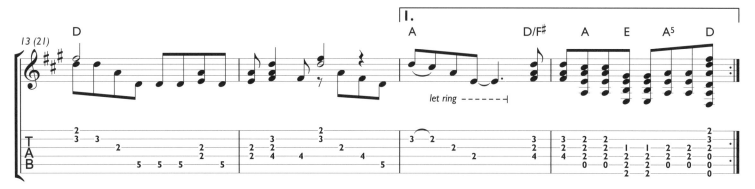

The love line is nev - er straight and nar - row,

Guitar solo

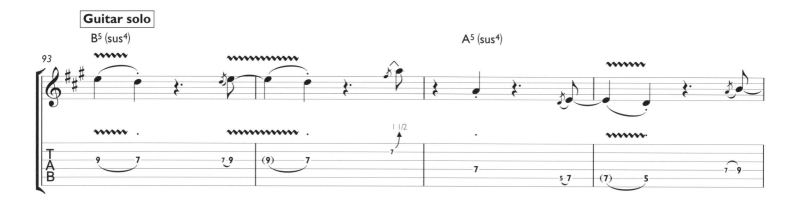

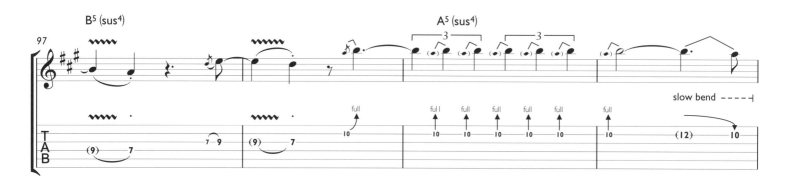

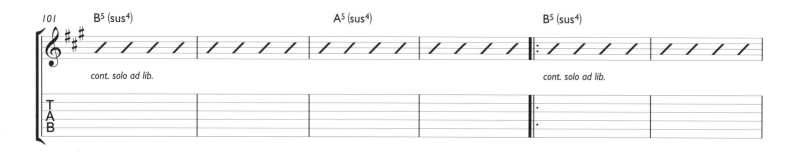

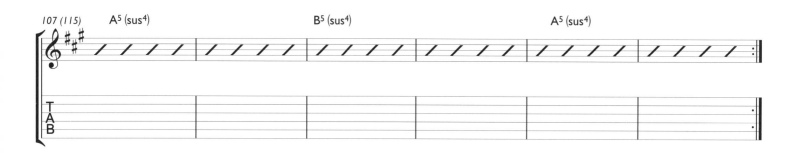

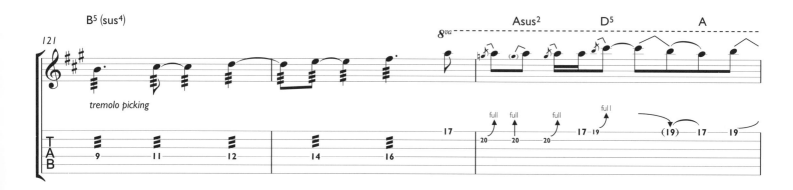

FREEWILL

Rush

Rush is a Canadian band that was formed in Toronto in 1968. Essentially a hard rock band, Rush's 40-year career has included a prog rock phase and a synthesiser period. Singer Geddy Lee's high vocal register provides an immediately identifiable sound. Guitarist Alex Lifeson's playing style is characterised by its use of different textures and complex rhythms and chord voicings. He once said 'Soloing shouldn't be about how fast or how many notes you can play…It's got to really relate to the song or be a reflection of something in your character.'

'Freewill' is from the band's 1980 album *Permanent Waves*. The lyrics of the song comprise a philosophical debate about free will, emphasising that it is not a gift but rather a choice.

'Freewill' should be played with moderate distortion; too much will make the full chords sound dissonant. Delay and chorus effects are also appropriate in this song – and boost is required for the guitar solo.

'Freewill' switches between different time signatures and tempi. This requires accurate counting and careful practice with the backing track. Bars 19–34 are in $\frac{2}{2}$ although the tempo remains the same as in the $\frac{4}{4}$ bars; you should feel two ♩ beats in a bar, rather than the four ♩ beats of $\frac{4}{4}$.

The second half (bars 67–74) of the guitar solo should be improvised. Make sure that you stay within the given style using, for example, pinch harmonics, whammy bends, and vibrato. You can write and memorise your solo or improvise it in the exam. Aim to make it develop in a logical and interesting way, as well as following the chord symbols.

'The *stars* aren't *aligned*, or *the* gods *are* malign'

RUN TO THE HILLS

Iron Maiden

Iron Maiden was formed in east London in 1976, taking its name from a medieval instrument of torture. They were one of the first bands of the new wave of British heavy metal to make any commercial impact. Throughout a career of more than three decades, Iron Maiden has been supported by 'Eddie' – a grotesque-looking monster-doll mascot.

'Run To The Hills' is from the album *The Number Of The Beast* (1982), which marked Bruce Dickinson's debut as lead vocalist and drummer Clive Burr's last album (he was replaced by Nicko McBrain). The song was written by bassist Steve Harris and features childhood friends Dave Murray and Adrian Smith both playing lead and rhythm guitar parts. The lyrics tell of the violence inflicted upon Native Americans in the 19th century. It has all the hallmarks of heavy metal – a loud, aggressive sound, with heavy guitar distortion, driving rhythms, and screaming vocals.

PERFORMANCE · HINTS & TIPS ·

'Run To The Hills' should be played with basic high gain valve ('Marshall') distortion. Avoid using too many effects, other than reverb, boost (required for the guitar solo) and the optional wah in bar 85.

Be sure to reach a true unison in the unison bends in bars 5–24 otherwise they will sound dissonant. Palm muting is used in verses 2 and 3, in bars 27–29 and 31–33.

The guitar solo (bars 85–100) incorporates many of Iron Maiden's stylistic trademarks, such as pinch harmonics, wide bar vibrato, and rapid HO/PO trills. Rhythmic accuracy is important in this solo, where the ♩ pulse is subdivided in several different ways, including into triplets. Practise this section slowly at first, aiming for a fluid sound when you play it at speed.

'Riding *through* dust *clouds* and *barren* wastes'

MAGGOT BRAIN

Funkadelic

Funkadelic was an ever-evolving funk collective under the leadership of George Clinton. The band started life supporting Clinton's doo-wop group, The Parliaments, but slowly morphed into Funkadelic. When the album *Maggot Brain* was recorded in 1971, the band comprised Eddie Hazel (guitar), Billy 'Bass' Nelson (bass), Tawl Ross (rhythm guitar), Bernie Warrell (keyboards) and Tiki Fulwood (drums).

Guitarist Eddie Hazel was born in Brooklyn in 1950. He grew up in Plainfield, New Jersey, where he joined Clinton's band. When recording the song 'Maggot Brain', Clinton asked Hazel to imagine the saddest possible thing for inspiration. According to legend, thinking of his mother's death led to Hazel's psychedelic extended guitar solo.

'Maggot Brain' should be played with distortion and wah or auto-wah. The lower volume of the intro can be achieved with guitar volume pot, volume pedal, or preset sound if using programmable multi-FX.

There is an opportunity to improvise in the intro, helping to create a psychedelic atmosphere for the opening of the song. The improvisation could be based on sonic effects (such as harmonics and volume swells), with or without melodic ideas, and should present a contrast with the rest of the song. You can write and memorise your solo, or improvise it in the exam.

Rhythmic accuracy is important in both the theme and the written solo, where the ♪ pulse is subdivided into several different types of groupings, including triplets. Practise this section slowly at first, aiming for a fluid sound when you play it at speed.

6:00

Dream Theater

Dream Theater is made up of three musicians who studied at the prestigious Berklee College of Music – school-friends John Petrucci (lead guitar) and John Myung (bass), and the drummer Mike Portnoy. Their music is often described as progressive metal – a style popular in the late 1980s and 1990s which combined the guitar-driven sounds of heavy metal with the more experimental and sophisticated compositions of prog rock.

Dream Theater, which drew its inspiration partly from Rush and Iron Maiden, is known for its high-energy live performances, technical proficiency and skilled musicianship. Guitarist John Petrucci is famous for his virtuosic playing style, which is characterised by his use of syncopation and complex rhythms.

'6:00' is taken from the 1994 album *Awake*.

'6:00' should be played with 'scooped' high gain distortion.

Although most of the song is in 4/4, there are several passages in 6/8 (bars 13–20, 57–64 and the Coda). The ♪ pulse remains the same throughout the changes of time signature – but be sure to be aware of the differences between 4/4 and 6/8.

Rhythmic accuracy is important throughout this song. Play all the ♪ notes evenly, taking particular care with the accents on the ♪ notes in bars 69–84. Although many of these accents fall into regular patterns, some are less predictable – so they need to be learnt carefully.

Bars 43 and 44 are quite complex. Bar 43 uses string skipping which should be practised slowly at first. The 'rapid fire' ♪ notes in bar 44 should be picked rather than slurred. In the link and chorus, you should use palm muting in order to avoid accidentally ringing open strings.

'Six *o'clock* and the siren *kicks* him *from* a *dream*'

THE CRYING MACHINE

Steve Vai

Steve Vai is a virtuosic rock guitarist who, in the 1980s, set new standards in technical ability. His playing is characterised by his use of rapid scales and arpeggios and his extensive exploration of effects, processors and the tremolo bar – all helping to create a wide variety of sounds.

Born in Long Island, Steve Vai studied guitar with his neighbour Joe Satriani, graduating from Berklee College of Music in 1979. As a teenager he transcribed one of Frank Zappa's technically demanding instrumentals and posted it to Zappa, along with a tape of his own playing. He was subsequently invited to tour with Zappa's band and went on to play with, amongst others, David Lee Roth and Whitesnake, before forming his own band in 1992.

'The Crying Machine' is taken from Vai's 1996 album *Fire Garden* which is divided into two parts – Phase 1 is nearly all instrumental while Phase II includes vocals.

Aim for 'creamy' high gain distortion but with enough high-frequency content for the operation of the wah to 'bite' at the toe position.

'The Crying Machine' incorporates several tremolo (or whammy bar) techniques – such as bar vibrato, dips and dive bombs. Take care with the intonation and make sure that you reach the target notes indicated: for example, when playing the dive bomb in bar 95, be sure to reach the final key note E. Other techniques important to this virtuosic style include bends, trills and pinch harmonics (in bar 10, for example).

ABOUT THE SONGS

5150

Van Halen

Van Halen was a Californian band formed by brothers Eddie Van Halen (guitar and keyboards) and Alex Van Halen (drums) in the 1970s. Their father was a musician and they both had classical training. One of the most successful heavy metal bands, Van Halen was renowned for loud distorted guitars, powerful bass riffs and flamboyant singing.

Van Halen was most successful during the 1980s, when the band was famous for its melodic hard-rock sound. During this period, the Van Halen brothers were joined by vocalist and rhythm guitarist Sammy Hagar and bass player Michael Anthony. '5150' is from Van Halen's 1986 album of the same name. The title refers to the band's home recording studio as well as to the custom-made electric guitar which Eddie Van Halen used throughout the 1980s.

Van Halen's advanced palette of techniques, such as two-handed tapping, tremolo picking, vibrato and harmonics, inspired a whole new generation of guitarists.

PERFORMANCE · HINTS & TIPS ·

'5150' should be played with high gain distortion, but not so much as to make the full chords sound dissonant. Boost is required for the guitar solo. Add stylistically appropriate techniques – such as pinch harmonics and vibrato – to your performance of the song.

Most of the rhythm work in '5150' should be lightly palm muted in order to avoid accidentally ringing open strings.

For this song, drop D tuning is required. This is very common in rock music, and means that the low E string is detuned down a tone to a D. You can do this by tuning it to the open D string (it will sound an octave lower), or by using the tuning notes on track 2 of the CD included with this book.

'The *love* line is never *straight* and *narrow*'

YOUR PAGE NOTES

SESSION SKILLS

PLAYBACK

For your exam, you can choose either Playback or Improvising (see page 46).
If you choose Playback, you will be asked to play some music you have not seen or heard before.

In the exam, you will be given the song chart and the examiner will play a recording of the music. You will hear several four-bar to eight-bar phrases on the recording: you should play each of them straight back in turn. There's a rhythm track going throughout, which helps you keep in time. There should not be any gaps in the music.

In the exam you will have two chances to play with the recording:
- First time – for practice
- Second time – for assessment

You should listen to the audio, copying what you hear; you can also read the music. Here are some practice song charts which are also on the CD in this book.

Don't forget that the Playback test can include requirements which may not be shown in these examples, including those from earlier grades. Check the parameters at www.trinityrock.com to prepare for everything which might come up in your exam.

'I really *like* the *way* music *looks* on *paper.* It *looks* like *art* to *me*'

Steve Vai

Practice playback 1

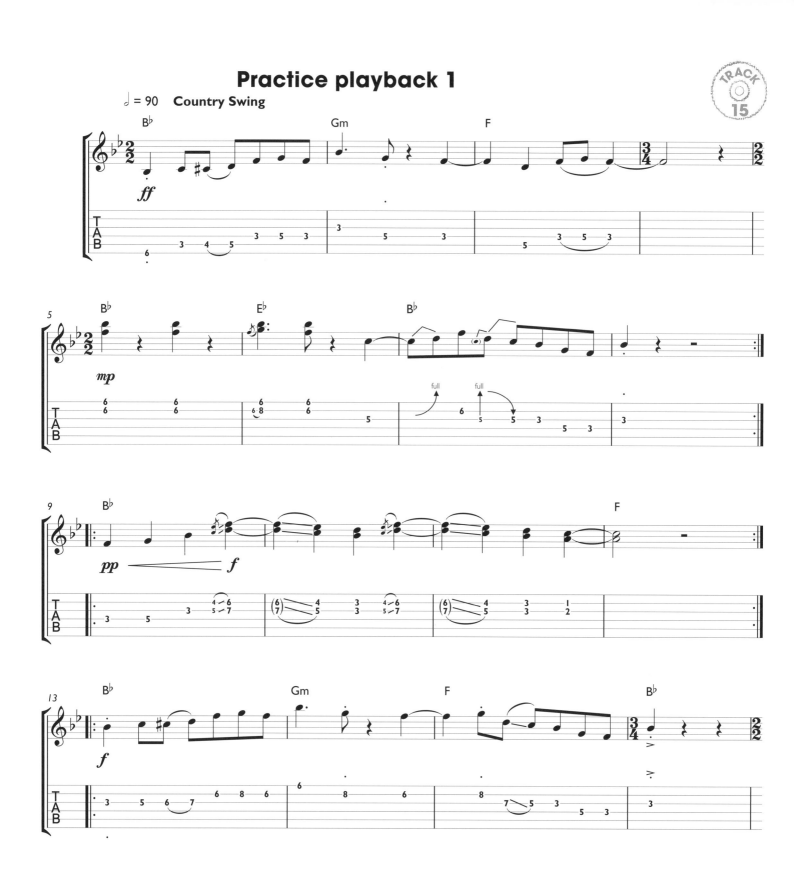

Practice playback 2

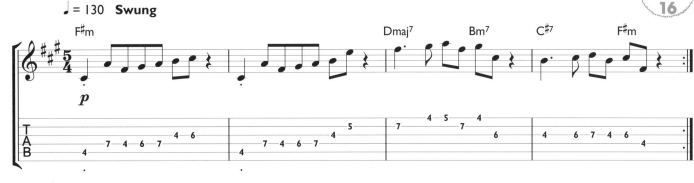

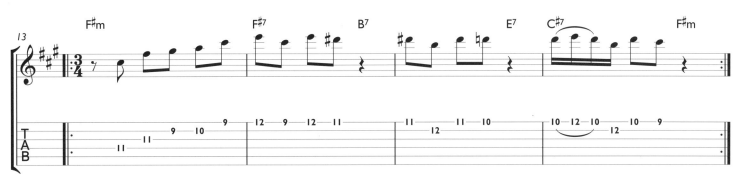

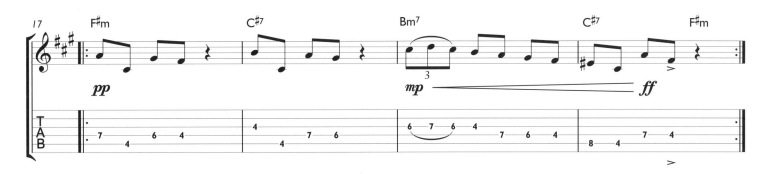

IMPROVISING

For your exam, you can choose either Playback (see page 43), or Improvising. If you choose to improvise, you will be asked to improvise over a backing track that you haven't heard before in a specified style.

In the exam, you will be given a song chart and the examiner will play a recording of the backing track. The backing track consists of a passage of music played on a loop. You can choose whether to play a lead melodic line, rhythmic chords, or a combination of the two.

In the exam you will have two chances to play with the recording:
- First time – for practice
- Second time – for assessment

Here are some improvising charts for practice which are also on the CD in this book.

Don't forget that the Improvising test can include requirements which may not be shown in these examples, including those from earlier grades. Check the parameters at www.trinityrock.com to prepare for everything which might come up in your exam.

Practice improvisation 1

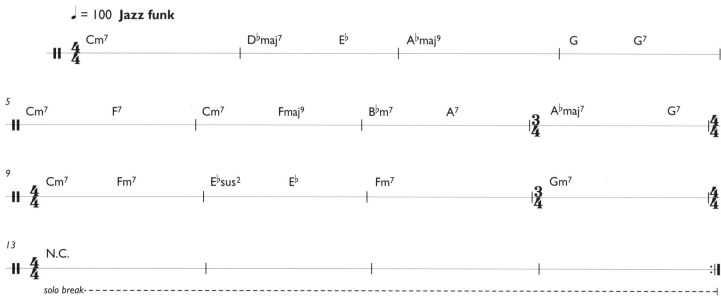

Practice improvisation 2

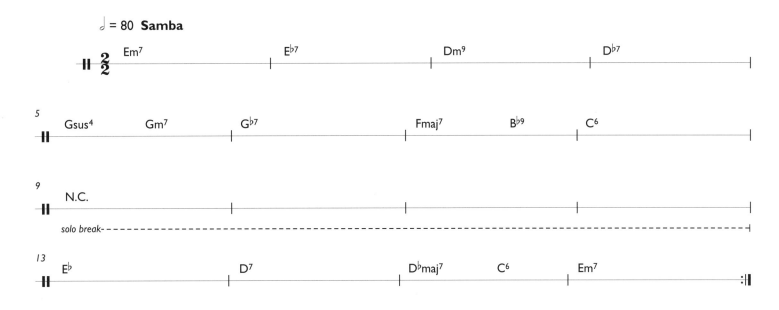

♩ = 80 **Samba**

2/2

| Em⁷ | E♭⁷ | Dm⁹ | D♭⁷ |

5
| Gsus⁴ | Gm⁷ | G♭⁷ | Fmaj⁷ | B♭⁹ | C⁶ |

9
N.C.

solo break

13
| E♭ | D⁷ | D♭maj⁷ | C⁶ | Em⁷ |

'Relax.
Enjoy yourself.
Play *a lot.*'

Joe Satriani

YOUR PAGE NOTES

CHOOSING A SONG FOR YOUR EXAM

There are lots of options to help you choose your three songs for the exam. For Songs 1 and 2, you can choose a song which is:

- from this book
- from www.trinityrock.com

Or for Song 2 you can choose a song which is:

- sheet music from a printed or online source.
- your own arrangement of a song or a song you have written yourself.

You can play the song unaccompanied or with a backing track (minus the guitar part). If you like, you can create a backing track yourself (or with friends), or you could add your own vocals – or both.

For Grade 8, the song should last between two-and-a-half and four minutes, and the level of difficulty should be similar to your other songs. When choosing a song, think about:

- Does it work on my instrument?
- Are there any technical elements that are too difficult for me?
- Do I enjoy playing it?
- Does it work with my other pieces to create a good set-list?

See www.trinityrock.com for further information and advice on choosing your own song.

SHEET MUSIC

For your exam, you must always bring an original copy of the book or download sheets with email certificate / proof of purchase for each song you perform in the exam. If you choose to write your own song you must provide the examiner with a copy of your music.
Your music can be:

- a lead sheet with lyrics, chords and melody line
- a chord chart with lyrics
- a full score using conventional staff/TAB notation

The title of the song and your name should be on the sheet music.

YOUR PAGE NOTES

IMPROVISING IN SONGS

Improvisation is an exciting and creative way to make the music your own. Rock and pop music often includes opportunities for musicians to improvise during a song – this is a great way to display your instrumental/vocal skills and musical abilities. This might include playing your own melody line, ad-libbing around a given tune or making up an accompaniment.

Make sure you know the song well and feel comfortable and confident with the rhythms, chord progressions and the general groove that underpins the music. Once you're familiar with it, the best way to learn how to improvise is to do it!

Some useful starting points might be:

* Identify just a few notes that sound good over the chord progressions, and experiment with these first.
* Add more notes as your musical ideas start to develop – improvising is often most effective when a simple idea is repeated, varied and extended.
* You don't need to fill every gap! Silence can be an important – and very effective – part of your improvisation.
* The more you improvise – and experiment – the better you will become, until your improvisations seem effortless.

It's important to be aware of the tonality of the song and to recognise different scales and modes that are appropriate to use. Start by familiarising yourself with:

* the minor pentatonic scale
* the blues scale
* the Dorian mode
* major and minor scales

You might find it useful to listen to some original versions of different rock and pop songs. Have a go at learning the solos that are played – this will help you to develop an understanding of how other musicians develop musical material.

PERFORMING

Being well prepared is the secret of a good performance. The more you practise, the better you will perform.

Top Ten Practice Tips

1 Develop a regular practice routine. Try to set aside a certain amount of time every day.

2 Choose specific things to practise each week.

3 Set goals for each practice session and continually review your progress.

4 Play a wide variety of songs – not just your favourites over and over again – to increase your skill and adaptability.

5 Identify the parts of the songs you find difficult and give them special attention.

6 Practise those techniques that you struggle with as well as those you find easier.

7 Don't reinforce mistakes by repeating them over and over again.

8 Include warm-ups and technical exercises in your practice sessions as well as songs.

9 Use a metronome.

10 Record yourself on audio or video. Listen to your older recordings to see how much you have improved.

Try to memorise the music – aim to sound free and natural and put your own stamp on the songs.

PERFORMING

BEFORE YOUR PERFORMANCE

- Watch and listen to others perform. Go to live performances and watch some videos online. Think about the aspects of performances you particularly like and try them out.
- Practise playing in front of an audience and communicate with them.
- Make sure your instrument is in good working order.
- Learn some relaxation and breathing exercises.
- Be positive about your performance. Think about how good your performance will be.
- Know your music.

ON THE DAY OF YOUR PERFORMANCE

- Wear something comfortable.
- Try some physical exercises.
- Warm up.
- Do some relaxation and breathing exercises.
- Make sure your instrument is in tune.

THE PERFORMANCE

Your audience may be large or small – and in an exam may only be one person – but it is important to give a sense of performance no matter how many people are present.

- Walk into the room confidently.
- Keep your head up, so you can look at your audience and acknowledge them.
- Focus on the music.
- Look confident and keep going, no matter what happens.
- Engage with your audience.
- Enjoy yourself.

YOUR PAGE

NOTES